A Moment With God

12-Month

Women's Devotional

DAMYTA JONES

A Moment With God 12-Month Devotional®
Copyright © 2018 by Damyta Jones
ISBN-13: 9781984303660
ISBN-10:198430366X

Dedication

This book is dedicated to all those special moments that I spent with God, my paper, and my pen.

—

Danyta Jones

FOREWARD

For years Damyta has been a beautiful spirit who took devotion with God very seriously. She is famous for writing and talking to God during her secret time with him. This book is a combination of her personal devotion and private study. If you want to be uplifted this book is for you. The devotional takes you on a one year journey to being encouraged by the word of God. She uses everyday examples coupled with godly wisdom to bring healing to the hearts of the people. This devotion will leave you basking in God's love for you. I encourage you to get ready for an overwhelming experience of God's love.

Prophetess Aja D. Jones

January

Stand for something. Make your life mean something. Start where you are with what you have. You are enough."
— Germany Kent

"You Are Enough"

Do you ever feel like you aren't doing anything right? I know I have felt this way many times. Some days I feel like I'm not a good mother or I'm not a good wife. I need to do this better and I need to do more of that. I'm not praying right, I don't fast correctly. I don't devote enough time to God or I don't read my bible enough. The enemy has tortured me with "You're just not good enough" for a long time. Ask yourself, not good enough for who? God loves us just the way we are. We can't escape his love. He works on us daily if we allow him to! He loves everything about us and he cares about what concerns us. This makes me thankful that he is continuing to work on me! So the next time you begin to feel like you can't do anything right, just know you are enough for Him. He's still working on his masterpiece in you!

Prayer

Dear Lord, help me to remember that you will not leave your work incomplete. Thank you for loving and working on me. In Jesus name. Amen.

W e e k   1

Philippians 1:6

I am convinced *and* confident of this
very thing, that He who has begun a
good work in you will [continue to]
perfect *and* complete it until the day of
Christ Jesus [the time of His return].

W e e k 2

2Corinthians 12:9-10

⁹ but He has said to me, "My grace is sufficient for you [My lovingkindness and My mercy are more than enough—always available—regardless of the situation]; for [My] power is being perfected [and is completed and shows itself most effectively] in [your] weakness." Therefore, I will all the more gladly boast in my weaknesses, so that the power of Christ [may completely enfold me and] may dwell in me. ¹⁰ So I am well pleased with weaknesses, with insults, with distresses, with persecutions, and with difficulties, for the sake of Christ; for when I am weak [in human strength], then I am strong [truly able, truly powerful, truly drawing from God's strength].

Week 3

Ephesians 2:10

¹⁰ For we are His workmanship [His own master work, a work of art], created in Christ Jesus [reborn from above—spiritually transformed, renewed, ready to be used] for good works, which God prepared [for us] beforehand [taking paths which He set], so that we would walk in them [living the good life which He prearranged and made ready for us].

Week 4

Romans 8:39

39 nor height, nor depth, nor any other created thing, will be able to separate us from the [unlimited] love of God, which is in Christ Jesus our Lord.

Deuteronomy 33:12

12 Of Benjamin he said,
"May the beloved of the LORD [a]dwell in safety by Him; He shields *and* covers him all the day long, And he dwells between His shoulders."

February

"Choices are the hinges of destiny."
—Edwin Markham
Decisions are a part of every believer's life. We must master the art of decision making if we want to succeed in life.

"Making Good Decisions"

As a mother there is so much work to be done. We wear several different hats. For those of us who are in the work field we are employees, we are mothers, wives, friends, daughters, sisters, and granddaughters. We have a place and position with each hat we wear. Being a mom is one of the most important jobs we have. We are in charge of taking care of and raising kids. That's a huge task! A part of raising kids is guiding them. One of my most quoted scriptures when talking with my daughter teaches about right and wrong. Genesis 4:7 is the story of Cain and Able. IN this verse God himself is talking to (warning) Cain about the consequences of choices. As a parent, we must take the time to explain things to our children. God is doing just that in this scripture. He is instructing Cain on the pros and cons of decisions. He explains the outcomes of doing what is right and doing what is wrong. I'm so thankful that God takes the time to guide his children. I use the scripture so much, my daughter knows where to pick up when I pause. It's important as we guide our children to explain things and be honest. Let them know there's a consequence to every decision.

Prayer

Dear Lord, please help me to make good decision making a legacy I leave for my kids to serve the next generation. Thank you for loving and guiding me. In Jesus name. Amen.

Week 1

Genesis 4:7

If you do well [believing Me and doing what is acceptable and pleasing to Me], will you not be accepted? And if you do not do well [but ignore My instruction], sin crouches at your door; its desire is for you [to overpower you], but you must master it."

Week 2

Proverbs 2:6

6 For the LORD gives [skillful and godly] wisdom; From His mouth come knowledge and understanding

Psalm 32:8

8 I will instruct you and teach you in the way you should go; I will counsel you [who are willing to learn] with My eye upon you.

Week 3

John 16:13

¹³ But when He, the Spirit of Truth, comes, He will guide you into all the truth [full and complete truth]. For He will not speak on His own initiative, but He will speak whatever He hears [from the Father—the message regarding the Son], and He will disclose to you what is to come [in the future].

Week 4

Psalm 119:105-106

105 Your word is a lamp to my feet
And a light to my path. 106 I have
sworn [an oath] and have confirmed
it, That I will keep Your righteous
ordinances.

March

"No is not a negative word. Sometimes saying no can save you from life's greatest pains."- Anonymous

"Saying No For The Better"

Being an adult and having to make
adult decisions really sucks sometimes.
You want to be present for everything
concerning your children but you can't.
Having to make decisions that hurt
your children's feelings are really hard.
You want to buy that thing they want
but you also have to have lights in
your home. You want to take them on
that vacation they have been wanting
to go on but you have to have a place
to stay. Sometimes we have to make
the better decision. Children don't
know if she buys me those shoes, we
won't have lights. If we go on that
vacation we will have to move. So
because of the wisdom and knowledge
we have sometimes we have to make
tough decisions for the better. God has
to do the same thing. Because of his
wisdom and knowledge he has to make
the better decision. We may want this
and want that which isn't a bad thing,

but it may cause some other issues down the road. so he make the better decision. That's why we just need to trust him. He knows all so what seems good to us and looks like the perfect set up may not be. It's hard to not have your feelings hurt when you are told no, but sometimes that no is for the best.

Prayer

Heavenly father thank you for wisdom. Thank you for giving us the wisdom to make the better decisions even when they are the hardest decisions. You know what's going to happen down the road so who's more trustworthy than you? I pray as you help us to also do what's better for our children that one day they will understand and appreciate our choices. In Jesus name I pray, Amen.

Week 1

Proverbs 3:5-6

Trust in *and* rely confidently on
the Lord with all your heart And do
not rely on your own
insight *or* understanding.[6]In all your
ways
know *and* acknowledge *and* recognize
Him,
And He will make your paths
straight *and* smooth [removing
obstacles that block your way].

W e e k   2

Proverbs 4:6-7

6 "Do not turn away from her
(Wisdom) and she will guard *and*
protect you; Love her, and she will
watch over you. 7 "The beginning of
wisdom is: Get [skillful and godly]
wisdom [it is preeminent]! And with
all your acquiring, get understanding
[actively seek spiritual discernment,
mature comprehension, and logical
interpretation].

Ecclesiastes 7:12

12 For wisdom is a protection *even as*
money is a protection, But the
[excellent] advantage of knowledge is
that wisdom shields *and* preserves the
lives of its possessors.

Week 3

James 1:5

⁵ If any of you lacks wisdom [to guide him through a decision or circumstance], he is to ask of [our benevolent] God, who gives to everyone generously and without rebuke *or* blame, and it will be given to him.

W e e k 4

Proverbs 19:20

²⁰ Listen to counsel, receive instruction,
and accept correction, That you may be
wise in the time to come.

April

Whatever you do [whatever your task may be], work from the soul [that is, put in your very best effort], as [something done] for the Lord and not for men
Colossians 3:23

"Work Is Never Done"

There is always work to be done. Whether it be with the kids, spouse, or your actual employment. There is always something to do! It's hard to find time for yourself. As a woman, we are always needed by someone and our first instinct is to take care of others first, then if there's time, tend to ourselves. It amazes me how God created us to be so much to so many and we actually do it. When I think about all God helps me to accomplish it leaves me speechless. Most days we do what we do without thinking about it. Take the time to think about all your responsibilities and everything you are in charge of and see how amazed you become because you get everything done. God is the reason we are able to do all these things and more. Read how the Proverbs woman does everything she does. All her tasks, jobs, responsibilities, and she handles them all with such grace and dignity. She is what most moms are today. Her example is one to follow and a great legacy to leave for our children. It's so important that we take our positions seriously because we play a huge part in the world and we influence so much.

Prayer

Heavenly father, thank you for the way you have created women. I pray you continue to supply all of our needs and we continue to raise and shape the future. Thank you for trusting us with so many precious things. Help us to fulfill the roles you have called us to in Jesus name we pray, Amen.

W e e k   1

Proverbs 31:10-31

An excellent woman [one who is
spiritual, capable, intelligent, and
virtuous], who is he who can find her?
Her value is more precious than
jewels *and* her worth is far above
rubies *or* pearls.[11] The heart of her
husband trusts in her [with secure
confidence],
And he will have no lack of gain.
[12] She comforts, encourages, *and* does
him only good and not evil All the
days of her life.[13] She looks for wool and
flax And works with willing hands in
delight.[14] She is like the merchant ships
[abounding with treasure];She brings
her [household's] food from far
away.[15] She rises also while it is still
night And gives food to her household
And assigns tasks to her maids.[16] She
considers a field before she
buys *or* accepts it [expanding her

business prudently];With her profits she plants fruitful vines in her vineyard.¹⁷ She equips herself with strength [spiritual, mental, and physical fitness for her God-given task]And makes her arms strong.
¹⁸ She sees that her gain is good; Her lamp does not go out, but it burns continually through the night [she is prepared for whatever lies ahead].
¹⁹ She stretches out her hands to the ᴵᵉ]distaff,
And her hands hold the spindle [as she spins wool into thread for clothing].²⁰ She opens *and* extends her hand to the poor,
And she reaches out her filled hands to the needy.²¹ She does not fear the snow for her household, For all in her household are clothed in [expensive] scarlet [wool].²² She makes for herself coverlets, cushions, *and* rugs of tapestry.
Her clothing is linen, pure *and* fine, and purple [wool].²³ Her husband is known in the [city's] gates, When he

sits among the elders of the land.²⁴ She makes [fine] linen garments and sells them; And supplies sashes to the merchants.²⁵ Strength and dignity are her clothing *and* her position is strong and secure;

And she smiles at the future [knowing that she and her family are prepared].²⁶ She opens her mouth in [skillful and godly] wisdom, And the teaching of kindness is on her tongue [giving counsel and instruction].²⁷ She looks well to how things go in her household, And does not eat the bread of idleness.²⁸ Her children rise up and call her blessed (happy, prosperous, to be admired);Her husband also, and he praises her, *saying,*²⁹ "Many daughters have done nobly, *and* well [with the strength of character that is steadfast in goodness],⁽ᶦ⁾But you excel them all."³⁰ Charm *and* grace are deceptive, and [superficial] beauty is vain, But a woman who fears the Lord [reverently worshiping, obeying, serving, and trusting Him with awe-filled respect], she shall be praised. [31] Give her of the product of her hands, And let her own works praise her in the gates [of the city].."

Week 2

Galatians 6:4-5

[4] But each one must carefully scrutinize his own work [examining his actions, attitudes, and behavior], and then he can have the personal satisfaction and inner joy of doing something commendable [a]without comparing himself to another. [5] For every person will have to bear [with patience] his own burden [of faults and shortcomings for which he alone is responsible].

Colossians 3:23-24

[23] Whatever you do [whatever your task may be], work from the soul [that is, put in your very best effort], as [something done] for the Lord and not for men, [24] knowing [with all certainty] that it is from the Lord [not from men] that you will receive the inheritance which is your [greatest]

reward. It is the Lord Christ whom you [actually] serve.

Week 3

Romans 14:10,12

¹⁰ But you, why do you criticize your brother? Or you again, why do you look down on your [believing] brother *or* regard him with contempt? For we will all stand before the judgment seat of God [who alone is judge].
¹² So then, each of us will give an account of himself to God.

Romans 14:15-16

¹⁵ If your brother is being hurt *or* offended because of food [that you insist on eating], you are no longer walking in love [toward him]. Do not let what you eat destroy *and* spiritually harm one for whom Christ died. ¹⁶ Therefore do not let what is a good thing for you [because of your freedom to choose] be spoken of as evil [by someone else];

W e e k   4

Proverbs 28:13

¹³ He who conceals his transgressions will not prosper, But whoever confesses and [a]turns away from his sins will find compassion *and* mercy.

2 Peter 1:10

¹⁰ Therefore, believers, be all the more diligent to make certain about His calling and choosing you [be sure that your behavior reflects and confirms your relationship with God]; for by [a]doing these things [actively developing these virtues], you will never stumble [in your spiritual growth and will live a life that leads others away from sin];

May

"Choices are the hinges of destiny."
—Edwin Markham
Decisions are a part of every
believer's life. We must master the
art of decision making if we want to
succeed in life.

"God Exists In The Mundane"

Do you ever feel like you are just going through the motion? Like you are just getting through day by day with nothing exciting or purposeful going on in your life. Oh my how I have felt this way many times. I still find myself feeling this way from time to time. We have to understand that nothing we do is without purpose when we are in the will of God. Understand that sometimes where he has us is not always glittery and shiny. We think of awesome things when we think of God, therefore we expect everything dealing with him must look like glitter and gold. With a mindset like this, we miss blessing in the mundane. You know the getting up before everyone else, getting ready to start your day, getting the kids up and ready for school, praying with them in the carpool line, getting to work and dealing with all sorts of messy, unhappy , rude and vindictive people, doing your best to make it through the day so you can get back home to your family. Helping kids with homework and projects, preparing dinner, all while giving your undivided attention to a toddler. Finally, getting everyone fed, bathed, and in bed just to get up and do it all over again. God will show himself to you right in the mundane. Like he did Moses while shepherding a flock of sheep. God showed up in a burning bush. When God is ready to reveal himself it may not come in a bed of roses but he just may show up in the middle of a messy day filled with rude people and a thousand demands. Just make sure you pay attention like Moses did and answer his call.

Prayer

Heavenly father, please forgive me when I overlook your grace and mercy because of my misconception of what things should look like. Allow me to also see your blessings no matter what my situation looks like. Help me to not miss you and to always answer your call. In Jesus name I pray, Amen.

W e e k 1
Exodus 3:1-6

Now Moses was keeping the flock of
Jethro (Reuel) his father-in-law, the
priest of Midian; and he led his flock to
the west side of the wilderness and
came to Horeb (Sinai), the mountain of
God. ²The [a]Angel of
the Lord appeared to him in a blazing
flame of fire from the midst of a bush;
and he looked, and behold, the bush
was on fire, yet it was not
consumed. ³So Moses said, "I must
turn away [from the flock] and see
this great sight—why the bush is not
burned up." ⁴When the Lord saw that
he turned away [from the flock] to
look, God called to him from the midst
of the bush and said, "Moses, Moses!"
And he said, "Here I am." ⁵Then God
said, "Do not come near; take your
sandals off your feet [out of respect],
because the place on which you are
standing is holy ground." ⁶Then He
said, "I am the God of your father, the
God of Abraham, the God of Isaac, and

the God of Jacob." Then Moses hid his face, because he was afraid to look at God.

Week 2

Jeremiah 29:11

[11] For I know the plans *and* thoughts
that I have for you,' says the LORD,
'plans for peace *and* well-being and not
for disaster, to give you a future and a
hope.

Week 3

1 John 3:1

3 See what an incredible quality of love the Father has shown to us, that we would [be permitted to] be named *and* called *and* counted the children of God! And so we are! For this reason the world does not know us, because it did not know Him.

Romans 5:8

8 But God clearly shows *and* proves His own love for us, by the fact that while we were still sinners, Christ died for us.

Week 4

Ephesians 2.4-7

⁴ But God, being [so very] rich in mercy, because of His great *and* wonderful love with which He loved us, ⁵ even when we were [spiritually] dead *and* separated from Him because of our sins, He made us [spiritually] alive together with Christ (for by His grace—His undeserved favor and mercy—you have been saved from God's judgment). ⁶ And He raised us up together with Him [when we believed], and seated us with Him in the heavenly *places*, [because we are] in Christ Jesus, ⁷ [and He did this] so that in the ages to come He might [clearly] show the immeasurable *and* unsurpassed riches of His grace in [His] kindness toward us in Christ Jesus [by providing for our redemption].

June

"Choices are the hinges of destiny." —Edwin Markham Decisions are a part of every believer's life. We must master the art of decision making if we want to succeed in life.

"Home Sweet Home"

Have you ever lived in a difficult environment? One where things are just falling apart every time you turn around? One thing after the other? I can relate to this on so many levels. My family and I have been experiencing this for years. We are at a point now where it's just getting worst. We have prayed and believed that God will bless us to move and start fresh. We've been in this situation for 9 years now. We have added another child to our family. I can't help but believe that the reason it's getting worst is because we are so close to our blessing! Many tests and trials are preparing us as God sees fit. To be honest this part of the process is very frustrating. Every time I look around something is broken, another issue has arisen, someone is acting a fool, and so on. It makes the fight very tiresome. When we go through these types of seasons, it's important to hold on and hang in there. This is a clear sign that help is on the way. Who want to fight so hard for so many years just to give up right when your blessing is within arm's reach? The enemy would love that. Trust in the Lord. Cast all your cares on him for he loves you. We must stay encouraged and trust in the Lord's process. I know one thing for sure, when our move is finalized I'm going to appreciate my new home more than any place we have lived before. This struggle has created in me a new humbleness towards having our own home. So many things I will not take for granted because of where we are coming from.

Prayer

Heavenly father, thank you for your love and wisdom. Thank you for the thorn that keeps us close to you. I pray you continue to carry us through the difficult process as our blessings are right in front of our face. Help us to hold on and not give up. In Jesus name I pray. Amen.

W e e k 1

Romans 5:3-4

³ And not only *this*, but [with joy] let us exult in our sufferings *and* rejoice in our hardships, knowing that hardship (distress, pressure, trouble) produces patient endurance; ⁴ and endurance, proven character (spiritual maturity); and proven character, hope *and* confident assurance [of eternal salvation].

Week 2

Joshua 1:9

9 Have I not commanded you? Be strong and courageous! Do not be terrified or dismayed (intimidated), for the LORD your God is with you wherever you go."

Romans 12:12

12 *constantly* rejoicing in hope [because of our confidence in Christ], steadfast *and* patient in distress, devoted to prayer [continually seeking wisdom, guidance, and strength],

Week 3

2 Samuel 7:28

²⁸ And now, O Lord GOD, You are God, and Your words are truth, and You have promised this good thing to Your servant.

Galatians 6:9

⁹ Let us not grow weary *or* become discouraged in doing good, for at the proper time we will reap, if we do not give in.

Week 4

Psalm 9:10

10 And those who know Your name [who have experienced Your precious mercy] will put their confident trust in You,
For You, O LORD, have not abandoned those who seek You.

Revelation 3:10

10 Because you have kept the word of My endurance [My command to persevere], I will keep you [safe] from the hour of trial, that *hour* which is about to come on the whole [inhabited] world, to test those who live on the earth.

July

"Choices are the hinges of destiny." —
Edwin Markham
Decisions are a part of every believer's
life. We must master the art of decision
making if we want to succeed in life.

"You Are Not The Driver"

Today I had a heart procedure done. I had a condititon called WPW, which causes me to have an irregular heart beat sometimes. My heart had an extra pathway to run on and you should only have one. This is something I was born with and at 35 I'm just now having symptoms. A procedure called an ablation can be done to burn off that extra pathway so that my heart's conduction can only go one way as it should. I begin to feel this strange feeling sometime after my son was born a year ago. I was surely concerned about this because I have loss three close relatives to heart issues. I knew I had to get this checked out and taken care of. After seeing my heart doctor he wanted me to have a heart cath done to perform the ablation. In the procedure, a catherter will be inserted through my thigh to my heart. They will look at my heart, find the spot, and burn it off. I have never had any type of procedure/surgery before. I've only birthed 2 children and that's about it! Now my mind is in total overload! This is my heart we are talking about! To say I was afraid was an understatement! One thing I was sure about was I have no control over this. You see, I'm the type who will worry , try to figure out, and try to fix a problem. I wear myself out and rarely have success when I do this. God knows when I'm in a situation that I fully understand there is no way I can do anything, I will let go. So that's just what I did, I let go. When I told people about my procedure, I would have a look on my face like there's nothing I can do and it was a sad face. Truth be told, I'm glad there was nothing I could do! I'm thankful I have a father who wants to take on all of my troubles! Who really doesn't want me to be burden with anything, but wants to give me everything! In my understanding that I'm not the driver, he is, I'm able to sit on the passenger side and take a nap! Needless to say my procedure went great! God's hands were all over me and everything went so well! I'm in awe of how great it all went! I find myself now being more conscience about trying to have the control. It's too much and it's so tiresome. I'm going to spend more time on the passenger side taking a nap or perhaps reading a good book!

Prayer

Heavenly father, thank you for your great love and mercy. Thank you for insisting that we give our burdens to you. Please forgive me when I insist on trying to handle everything knowing I'm not capapble. Lord help me to remember that I must follow you. In Jesus name I pray, Amen.

Week 1
Mark 8: 34-35

34 Jesus called the crowd together with His disciples, and said to them, "If anyone wishes to follow Me [as My disciple], he must deny himself [set aside selfish interests], and [a]take up his cross [expressing a willingness to endure whatever may come] and follow Me [believing in Me, conforming to My example in living and, if need be, suffering or perhaps dying because of faith in Me]. 35 For whoever wishes to save his life [in this world] will [eventually] lose it [through death], but whoever loses his life [in this world] for My sake and the gospel's will save it [from the consequences of sin and separation from God].

W e e k   2

Colossians 3:2

² Set your mind *and* keep focused *habitually* on the things above [the heavenly things], not on things that are on the earth [which have only temporal value].

Week 3

Isaiah 43:18

[18] "Do not remember the former things,
Or ponder the things of the past.

Week 4

Philippians 3:13-14

13 [e]Brothers and sisters, I do not consider that I have made it my own yet; but one thing *I do*: forgetting what *lies* behind and reaching forward to what *lies* ahead, 14 I press on toward the goal to win the [heavenly] prize of the upward call of God in Christ Jesus.

Proverbs 4:25-27

25 Let your eyes look directly ahead [toward the path of moral courage] And let your gaze be fixed straight in front of you [toward the path of integrity]. 26 Consider well *and* watch carefully the path of your feet, And all your ways will be steadfast *and* sure. 27 Do not turn away to the right nor to the left [where evil may lurk]; Turn your foot from [the path of] evil.

August

"Choices are the hinges of destiny."
— Edwin Markham
Decisions are a part of every
believer's life. We must master the
art of decision making if we want to
succeed in life.

"The Waging War"

The love of God is like nothing you've ever experienced once you experience it! For me personally, I find myself reflecting back on things God has done and worked out in my life and it blows my mind how much he loves me! At the sametime I often forget how much he loves me. Isn't that strange? It's a daily struggle when you are wrestling against the flesh and the spirit. The bible tells us that the battle against the flesh and spirit is a daily battle! That means everyday we will find ourselves fighting this war! As a Christian, I can testify to this being true. On the one hand we are spiritually aware and connected to God and we recognize his presence in ourlives. On the other, as we live in this world and struggle with being different and fight against culture, it's easy to fall prey to our society. This is why we have to connect with God every single day! We have to communicate with him, we have to keep in close relationship with him. We can't fall off our daily worship and praise for him. This is what helps fight the battle! This is how the spirit can over power the flesh! If we get relaxed with our daily connection to him, we will begin to see the flesh over power the spirit! God has already made us aware of this through scripture. Let's pay close attention to his word so we don't miss the warnings that will help us lead a successful life!

Prayer

Heavenly father, thank you for your love. The type of love that knows no bounds! The type of love that wants to fully protect and keep your children safe. Help us to have great discernment so we don't miss your signs and warnings that are for our great protection! In Jesus name I pray, Amen!

Week 1

Galatians 5:16-18

16 But I say, walk *habitually* in the
[Holy] Spirit [seek Him and be
responsive to His guidance], and then
you will certainly not carry out the
desire of the [a]sinful nature [which
responds impulsively without regard
for God and His precepts]. 17 For the
sinful nature has its desire which is
opposed to the Spirit, and the [desire
of the] Spirit opposes the [b]sinful
nature; for these [two, the sinful
nature and the Spirit] are in direct
opposition to each other [continually
in conflict], so that you [as believers]
do not [always] do whatever [good
things] you want to do. 18 But if you
are guided *and* led by the Spirit, you
are not subject to the Law.

Week 2
2 Corinthians 10:3-5

³ For though we walk in the flesh [as mortal men], we are not carrying on our [spiritual] warfare according to the flesh *and* using the weapons of man. ⁴ The weapons of our warfare are not physical [weapons of flesh and blood]. Our weapons are divinely powerful for the destruction of fortresses. ⁵ *We are* destroying sophisticated arguments and every exalted *and* proud thing that sets itself up against the [true] knowledge of God, and *we are* taking every thought *and* purpose captive to the obedience of Christ,

Week 3

Isaiah 54:17

[17] "No weapon that is formed against you will succeed; And every tongue that rises against you in judgment you will condemn. This [peace, righteousness, security, and triumph over opposition] is the heritage of the servants of the LORD, And *this is* their vindication from Me," says the LORD.

John 16:33

[33] I have told you these things, so that in Me you may have [perfect] peace. In the world you have tribulation *and* distress *and* suffering, but be courageous [be confident, be undaunted, be filled with joy]; I have overcome the world." [My conquest is accomplished, My victory abiding.]

Week 4
Ephesians 6:11-17

11 Put on the full armor of God [for His precepts are like the splendid armor of a heavily-armed soldier], so that you may be able to [successfully] stand up against all the schemes *and* the strategies *and* the deceits of the devil. 12 For our struggle is not against flesh and blood [contending only with physical opponents], but against the rulers, against the powers, against the world forces of this [present] darkness, against the spiritual *forces* of wickedness in the heavenly (supernatural) *places.* 13 Therefore, put on the complete armor of God, so that you will be able to [successfully] resist *and* stand your ground in the evil day [of danger], and having done everything [that the crisis demands], to stand firm [in your place, fully prepared, immovable, victorious]. 14 So

stand firm *and* hold your ground, HAVING [a]TIGHTENED THE WIDE BAND OF TRUTH (personal integrity, moral courage) AROUND YOUR WAIST and HAVING PUT ON THE BREASTPLATE OF RIGHTEOUSNESS (an upright heart), [15] and having [b]strapped on YOUR FEET THE GOSPEL OF PEACE IN PREPARATION [to face the enemy with firm-footed stability and the readiness produced by the good news]. [16] Above all, lift up the [protective] [c]shield of faith with which you can extinguish all the flaming arrows of the evil *one*. [17] And take THE HELMET OF SALVATION, and the sword of the Spirit, which is the Word of God.

September

"Choices are the hinges of destiny." —
Edwin Markham
Decisions are a part of every believer's life.
We must master the art of decision making
if we want to succeed in life.

"I'm Tired"

There are times in my life when I'm just tired. Sometimes my tiredness is physical. I just feel like I need to rest. My body is alerting me that I have done enough. Sometimes my tiredness is mental. My brain constantly runs and never seems to stop. I'm always trying to figure out how to get out of the mess I'm in or how am I going to take care of this or that. I'm consistantly trying to figure out a solution to the problem. Other times I'm emotionally tired. My emotions are all over the place and it drains me. I'm feeling like this one day and like that the other. As a young wife and mother, many of my days are emotionally stressful. I'm so thankful the word of God tells me when I'm tired He gives me strength! God knows his creation and he knows we can only go so far and for so long before we wear out! I love that he always has us in mind. So even on your weakest day, God will give you new strength so you can soar like eagles!

Prayer

Heavenly father, please help me to remember that I can't do it all. When I run low on strength replenish and refresh me so that I can continue to run the race. Thank you for always having me in mind. In Jesus name I pray, Amen.

W e e k 1

Isaiah 40:29-31

²⁹ He gives strength to the weary,
And to him who has no might He
increases power. ³⁰ Even youths grow
weary and tired,
And vigorous young men stumble
badly, ³¹But those who wait for the
LORD [who expect, look for, and hope
in Him] Will gain new strength *and*
renew their power; They will lift up
their wings [and rise up close to God]
like eagles [rising toward the sun];
They will run and not become weary,
They will walk and not grow tired.

Week 2

Philippians 4:13

¹³ I can do all things [which He has called me to do] through Him who strengthens *and* empowers me [to fulfill His purpose—I am self-sufficient in Christ's sufficiency; I am ready for anything and equal to anything through Him who infuses me with inner strength and confident peace.]

Psalm 119:28

²⁸ My soul dissolves because of grief; Renew *and* strengthen me according to [the promises of] Your word.

Week 3

2Corinthians 12.9-10

9 but He has said to me, "My grace is sufficient for you [My lovingkindness and My mercy are more than enough—always available—regardless of the situation]; for [My] power is being perfected [and is completed and shows itself most effectively] in [your] weakness." Therefore, I will all the more gladly boast in my weaknesses, so that the power of Christ [may completely enfold me and] may dwell in me. 10 So I am well pleased with weaknesses, with insults, with distresses, with persecutions, and with difficulties, for the sake of Christ; for when I am weak [in human strength], then I am strong [truly able, truly powerful, truly drawing from God's strength].

Psalm 28:7-8

⁷ The Lord is my strength and my [impenetrable] shield; My heart trusts [with unwavering confidence] in Him, and I am helped; Therefore my heart greatly rejoices,
And with my song I shall thank Him and praise Him. ⁸ The Lord is their [unyielding] strength, And He is the fortress of salvation to His anointed.

Week 4

Psalm 46:1

46 God is our refuge and strength
[mighty and impenetrable], A very
present *and* well-proved help in
trouble.

Ephesians 3:16

[16] May He grant you out of the riches
of His glory, to be strengthened *and*
spiritually energized with power
through His Spirit in your inner self,
[indwelling your innermost being and
personality],

October

"Choices are the hinges of destiny." — Edwin Markham
Decisions are a part of every believer's life. We must master the art of decision making if we want to succeed in life.

"Where's the love"

The present time we are in is getting darker and darker. People are doing whatever they want! Whatever makes them feel good is what they are doing. The bible warns us about being led by our feelings! It says the heart is deceitful. Being led by our feelings has our world in turmoil. We are killing each other, we are killing our children, we are hating one another and it makes for a hard world to live in. Jesus tells us what it all boils down to; the two most important commandments to abide by. Love God with all your heart, soul, and mind and love your neighbor as yourself! We simply need to love! The bible tells us that love covers a multitude of sins! God loved us so much he put together a well thought plan to free us from sin and come to a relationship with him! He did this out of his great love for us. Love seperates us from everyone else! Jesus said "by this everyone will know that you are my disciples, if you love one another." Love is so powerful it changes lives!

The empact that love can have on one's life is tremendous! We can change the world through love alone! We need to love each other back to life because we are living in a dying world!

Prayer

Dear Lord, please forgive us when we don't look like you or love like you! It's hard to do sometimes with the condition the world is in. Please help us to do as you have commanded so we can make a true difference in this world. In Jesus name I pray, Amen.

Week 1
1 John 4: 10-12

¹⁰ In this is love, not that we loved God, but that He loved us and sent His Son to be the propitiation [that is, the atoning sacrifice, and the satisfying offering] for our sins [fulfilling God's requirement for justice against sin and placating His wrath]. ¹¹ Beloved, if God so loved us [in this incredible way], we also ought to love one another. ¹² No one has seen God at any time. But if we love one another [with unselfish concern], God abides in us, and His love [the love that is His essence abides in us and] is completed *and* perfected in us.

Week 2

John 13:34

34 I am giving you a new commandment, that you [a]love one another. Just as I have loved you, so you too are to love one another.

Leviticus 19:18

18 You shall not take revenge nor bear any grudge against the sons of your people, but you shall love your neighbor (acquaintance, associate, companion) as yourself; I am the LORD.

Week 3

1 Peter 4:8

⁸ Above all, have [a]fervent *and* unfailing love for one another, because love covers a multitude of sins [it overlooks unkindness and unselfishly seeks the best for others].

Romans 13:8

⁸ [a]Owe nothing to anyone except to [b]love *and* seek the best for one another; for he who [unselfishly] loves his neighbor has fulfilled the [essence of the] law [relating to one's fellowman].

Week 4

1 John 3:18

18 Little children (believers, dear ones), let us not love [merely in theory] with word or with tongue [giving lip service to compassion], but in action and in truth [in practice and in sincerity, because practical acts of love are more than words].

Ephesians 4:2

2 with all humility [forsaking self-righteousness], and gentleness [maintaining self-control], with patience, bearing with one another [a]in [unselfish] love

November

"Choices are the hinges of destiny." — Edwin Markham
Decisions are a part of every believer's life. We must master the art of decision making if we want to succeed in life.

"My Help"

There was this one particular day that I remember struggling with financial issues. On this day as I was dealing with this issue, God put a song on my heart. The verse that played over and over in my mind was "I lift my eyes up my help comes from the Lord." I knew God was speaking to me. See, my commons sense told me, you need money because you have money problems. That makes good sense doesn't it? God was telling me I need him because He is my help. Then he lead me to Psalm 37:39-40 which starts off by saying "The salavation of the righteous come from the Lord." Salvation means preservation or deliverance from harm, ruin, or loss. I love when God speaks to me! My situation that I was dealing with, he gave me the solution to the problem. I thought all I need is money to fix the money problem, while my father said no I want to deliver you from this harm, this ruin, this loss! My thoughts were on a temporary fix, but God's plan is to get rid of it completely! He always has a bigger and better plan! Stop searching for a temporary fix and search for God for complete deliverance! He wants us out of the pit, not constantly jumping back and forth in it!

Prayer

Heavenly father, thank you for your grace and mercy. Thank you for always wanting the best for your children. Please forgive me when I think I know better than you. I pray that I always take heed to your voice and be obedient to your instructions. Although my thoughts are on temporary, yours are always on full completeness! Continue to lead me to my better. In Jesus name I pray, Amen.

W e e k 1

Psalm 37:39-40

[38] As for transgressors, they will be completely destroyed; The future of the wicked will be cut off. [39]But the salvation of the righteous is from the LORD; He is their refuge *and* stronghold in the time of trouble. [40]The LORD helps them and rescues them; He rescues them from the wicked and saves them, Because they take refuge in Him.

Week 2

Psalms 54:4

[4] Behold, God is my helper *and* ally;
The Lord is the sustainer of my soul
[my upholder].

Psalms 121:1-8

The LORD the Keeper of Israel. A Song
of [a]Ascents. [1] I will lift up my eyes to
the hills [of Jerusalem]—From where
shall my help come? [2] My help comes
from the LORD, Who made heaven and
earth. [3] He will not allow your foot to
slip; He who keeps you will not
slumber. [4] Behold, He who keeps Israel
Will neither slumber [briefly] nor
sleep [soundly]. [5] The LORD is your
keeper; The LORD is your shade on
your right hand. [6] The sun will not
strike you by day, Nor the moon by
night. [7] The LORD will protect you
from all evil; He will keep your life. [8]
The LORD will guard your going out
and your coming in [everything that

you do] From this time forth and forever.

Week 3

Isaiah 41:10

10 'Do not fear [anything], for I am
with you;
Do not be afraid, for I am your God.
I will strengthen you, be assured I will
help you; I will certainly take hold of
you with My righteous right hand [a
hand of justice, of power, of victory, of
salvation].

Hebrews13:5-6

5 Let your character [your moral
essence, your inner nature] be free
from the love of money [shun greed—
be financially ethical], being content
with what you have; for He has said, "I
WILL NEVER [under any
circumstances] DESERT YOU [nor give
you up nor leave you without support,
nor will I in any degree leave you
helpless], NOR WILL I FORSAKE *or* LET
YOU DOWN *or* RELAX MY HOLD ON YOU
[assuredly not]!" 6 So we take comfort

and are encouraged *and* confidently say, "The Lord is my Helper [in time of need], I will not be afraid.
What will man do to me?"

Deuteronomy 31:6

⁶ Be strong and courageous, do not be afraid or tremble in dread before them, for it is the LORD your God who goes with you. He will not fail you or abandon you."

Week 4

1 Peter 2:9

9 But you are A CHOSEN RACE, A royal
PRIESTHOOD, A CONSECRATED NATION,
A [special] PEOPLE FOR *God's* OWN
POSSESSION, so that you may proclaim
the excellencies [the wonderful deeds
and virtues and perfections] of Him
who called you out of darkness into
His marvelous light.

John 14:26

26 But the [a]Helper (Comforter,
Advocate, Intercessor—Counselor,
Strengthener, Standby), the Holy
Spirit, whom the Father will send in
My name [in My place, to represent
Me and act on My behalf], He will
teach you all things. And He will help
you remember everything that I have
told you.

Psalm 118:7

7The Lord is on my side, He is among those who help me; Therefore I will look [in triumph] on those who hate me.

December

"Choices are the hinges of destiny." — Edwin Markham

Decisions are a part of every believer's life. We must master the art of decision making if we want to succeed in life.

"Did you say free?"

Do you know how excited we get when we are offered something free? Whatever we need to do to get it, we will do! Free in this day and time is a rare commodity. Everything you get nowadays comes with a price. Thus, the cycle of the economy! We work to make money, then we get paid to spend the money! Working is hard and it requires a lot of our time. Spending money is quick and easy. It takes way more time to make the money than it takes to spend it! This is why when we hear the word free, we jump on it! The way our world is today we are influenced by culture and that keeps us from the things that are truly important. Culture tells us to always want more, to be selfish, to never be satisfied, to love money, and many other wrong things! Culture also teaches the more expensive it is, the better the quality. Being wrapped up in the web of lies, we often forget and make less of the free gift offered to every single person on earth. The free gift of salvation that secures our eternity! Which comes with the bonus of grace and mercy, which by the way are also free! These free gifts that our culture over looks and devalues on a daily bases, are real important things that we allow the enemy to distract us from! To the point of being too late for some. We must remove the scales from our eyes and see the real trick that's in front of our faces! Satan wants as many as he can get! He knows distraction is going to take out a lot of us! Let's stay woke! Do not let him make light of the most expensive free gift that is out there! We all need to jump on this and make sure we are telling everyone about it so they don't miss out!

Prayer

Heavenly father, thank you for your Son Jesus! Thank you for his sacrifice that saved the world. My prayer is that we share the good news with others so they don't miss the opportunity to be a part of your kingdom through salvation. Thank you for making it so easy to accept and even more easier to purchase because it's free. Your love for us produced a well thought out plan to save us and to have a relationship with us. Thank you for everything you do! In Jesus name I pray, Amen.

W e e k 1

Romans 10:9-10

⁹ because if you acknowledge *and* confess with your mouth that Jesus is Lord [recognizing His power, authority, and majesty as God], and believe in your heart that God raised Him from the dead, you will be saved. ¹⁰ For with the heart a person believes [in Christ as Savior] resulting in his justification [that is, being made righteous—being freed of the guilt of sin and made acceptable to God]; and with the mouth he acknowledges *and* confesses [his faith openly], resulting in *and* confirming [his] salvation.

Week 2

Romans 3:23

⁹ because if you acknowledge *and*
confess with your mouth that Jesus is
Lord ⌜recognizing His power,
authority, and majesty as God⌝, and
believe in your heart that God raised
Him from the dead, you will be saved.
¹⁰ For with the heart a person believes
⌜in Christ as Savior⌝ resulting in his
justification ⌜that is, being made
righteous—being freed of the guilt of
sin and made acceptable to God⌝; and
with the mouth he acknowledges *and*
confesses ⌜his faith openly⌝, resulting
in *and* confirming ⌜his⌝ salvation.

Hebrews 7:25

²⁵ Therefore He is able also to save
forever (completely, perfectly, for
eternity) those who come to God
through Him, since He always lives to

intercede *and* intervene on their behalf [with God].

Week 3

Acts 4:12

¹² And there is salvation in no one else; for there is no other name under heaven that has been given among people by which we must be saved [for God has provided the world no alternative for salvation]."

Acts 16:31

³¹ And they answered, "Believe in the Lord Jesus [as your personal Savior and entrust yourself to Him] and you will be saved, you and your household [if they also believe]."

Acts 2:21

²¹ 'And it shall be that everyone who calls upon the name of the Lord [invoking, adoring, and worshiping the Lord Jesus] shall be saved (rescued spiritually).

Week 4

2Timothy1:9

⁹ for He delivered us *and* saved us and called us with a holy calling [a calling that leads to a consecrated life—a life set apart—a life of purpose], not because of our works [or because of any personal merit—we could do nothing to earn this], but because of His own purpose and grace [His amazing, undeserved favor] which was granted to us in Christ Jesus before the world began [eternal ages ago],

1) *Luke 19:10*

¹⁰ for the Son of Man has come to seek and to save that which was lost."

F i n a l
T h o u g h t s

The completion of this devotional has
been quite the journey! I never thought
my personal time with the Lord would
produce a book. Years of writing my
thoughts and prayers along with
scripture turned out to be the perfect
recipe for what God planned to birth
through me. I'm so grateful and
thankful to God for allowing me to do
something I never thought I could do
or ever considered. See that's what He
does, he will do a work in you that's
not like anything you are capable of
doing on your own just so that you
know where your help comes from. In
the process, He gets all the glory! This
has been an amazing experience to see
years of my life come together on the
pages of a book! My hope is that my
experiences and struggles will
encourage someone and show them
that with Christ we can get through

anything! If nothing else, please remember the importance of spending time with God because you never know what He has planned for you!!

CPSIA information can be obtained
at www.ICGtesting.com
Printed in the USA
BVHW051018231222
654934BV00011B/193